Hoc loco habitat fortuna,
hic quiescit cor.

In this place abideth happiness,
here the heart findeth peace

Marianus Mayer

Ammergau Alps
Meditation Trail

Content

Prologue 11

The 15 stations
1 Pilgrimage Church of Wies (Wieskirche) 20
2 Rottenbuch Abbey (Kloster Rottenbuch) 22
3 Lake Soier (Soier See) 24
4 Scheibum 26
5 Fatima Chapel (Fatimakapelle) 28
6 Rochusfeld 30
7 Kappel Church (Kappelkirche) 32
8 Hörnle 34
9 Passion Play Theatre (Passionstheater) 36
10 Monument of Crucifixion (Kreuzigungsgruppe) 38
11 Döttenbichl 40
12 Ettal Abbey (Kloster Ettal) 42
13 Ammer springs (Ammerquellen) 44
14 Gertrudis Chapel (Gertrudiskapelle) 46
15 Linderhof Palace (Schloss Linderhof) 48

Directions 51

Sponsors of the Meditation Trail 80
Symbolism of the 15 stations 82
Information centres 83
Map 85

Prologue

Living in the mountains was and is surely a dream of many a city dweller or lowlands inhabitant. A dream that has quite a few facets. One of these facets was the notion of a great number of visitors from the northern regions, such as Lübeck-born Thomas Mann for example, who spent his holidays in Oberammergau, that Bavaria was a type of Italy, due to its joie de vivre. Ludwig Ganghofer continued to awaken the Germans' interest and enthusiasm for the Ammergau Alps and its wonderful people with his bestseller "Der Herrgottschnitzer von Ammergau" (The Crucifix Carver of Ammergau) in 1880. Even the Imperial Court in Berlin was taken in by his ideas of a happier, more natural and creative life in this region, saturated with tradition and so in touch with nature.

The towns and villages in the region would like to invite you to the mountains, the Ammergau Alps, for meditative walking tours, and a whole lot more than tourist sights: paths leading to mental and spiritual impulses. This might at first seem strange to those who see the foothills and high country of the Alps merely as rustic Bavarian "Lederhosen" terrain or as a fun park for various types of sport, and believing that spiritual stimulus belongs in Indian ashrams or sweat lodges of native Americans. However, those who are keen to discover and are free of prejudices may take up our offer to find out more about the human presence hidden in the spiritual stores with regard to the region's arts and culture, to learn more about themselves through the testimonies of centuries they come across at every turn, and to gain knowledge of what our splendid nature and, last but not least, the local people may reveal through legacies and reflections of any kind.

It would be immodest to expect to immediately experience the elated feeling reflected in the words carved into a glass window in the Pilgrimage Church of Wies by the abbot Marianus Mayer, who was responsible for the construction of the Pilgrimage Church of Wies, on completion of such a walking trail: "Hoc loco habitat fortuna, hic quiescit cor.", meaning "In this place abideth happiness, here the heart findeth peace". This was, after all, quite a provocative assumption when considering that the author of these lines must have been thinking of the words by Augustinus, in his great quest for God and the truth: "Inquietum cor nostrum, donec requiescat in te. – Restless is our heart until it finds its peace in you". On the one hand, Augustinus' sentence, which appears at the beginning of his reflection on centuries of detours and meanders, makes us realise that the paths we must walk may be longer than those in the Ammergau Alps. On the other hand, he is referring to the starting point, the restrictions we want to break free from: we are restless, not at peace with ourselves, not truly self-conscious, not able to be completely by ourselves, nor be there for others, not to mention even others. Would it help to start the journey through the mountains?

In general, timeout and breaks from daily routine most certainly help, similar to the moments taken by an artist to step back from his easel to check the latest stage of his work. The fact that the remote – relatively speaking – valleys in the Ammergau Alps are well suited for this type of reflection can be seen in the concentration of monasteries in the region, such as Ettal Abbey, the Benedictine monastery nestled in a gap between two mountain ranges. Besides being a facility for ever-renewed orientation to the Bethlehemian fixed star, it is also an attempt to link heaven and earth. The fact that these and other Benedictine settlements, as well as the great Abbey of Monte Cassino, can be found on hills is proof that the members of the order hoped that this location would be beneficial to spiritual life. Can we find reasons for this?

What is however extraordinary, is that significant religious acts took place on or in the mountains, for example Moses' thorn bush

The Graswang Valley

encounter and the acceptance of the Law at Sinai, or the sermon on the mount. And is Jerusalem not the archetype of a city on a mountain – curiously enough, at the same altitude as Oberammergau. Those who have experienced the mountains, even if only when climbing the Oberammergau landmark Kofel, will know that everyday life becomes a little less significant and the appreciation of the essential gains in importance. And the higher the climb, the more extensive the sky. To reach for the infinite and becoming expansive by gazing into the immeasurable expanse – can that not be classified as a type of religious experience? It is not without reason that crosses are erected on summits and mountain mass services are held here, too.

At the same time, when out in nature, one begins to question himself. Why is it that we find nature so appealing? Why does it affect us? To what extent are we part of it and simultaneously also something else? When in the mountains, we occupy ourselves with

questions such as these, both on a physical and on a spiritual level. And there are consequences. Perhaps even those described by retired Bishop Stecher from Innsbruck: "Many paths lead to God. One of them is over the mountains."

The first European to climb a mountain for no practical reasons whatsoever, the poet Petrarca, concerned himself with thoughts of a very different nature when he summitted

Mont Ventoux on 26 April 1336, namely thoughts of severe self-doubt. He reproached himself for having forgotten the Creator in marvelling over his creation. To calm his conscience he took out the book he had carried along on his mountain tour, the previously mentioned autobiography of Augustinus, and was taken aback when he came across the following sentence: "And man goes to admire the heights of the mountains and the powerful tides in the sea and the flow of the widest streams and the currents of the ocean and the stars in the orbit – and in so doing loses himself." So, who has gauged the prospects and risks associated with mountains correctly – the Bishop or Petrarca and Augustinus? Hiking trails in the Ammergau Alps provide an opportunity to question this personally.

Cultural stations along the route may also be places of spiritual, meditative involvement. We need look no further than Knoller's picture of The Holy Family in Ettal Abbey for example, whose faces exude inner light, or some of the figures in the large manger in the Oberammergau Museum. Many sculptures whose gestures and postures are representative of spiritual attitude are also worthwhile objects for meditation: another indicator of how deep the belief truly was here. The wanderer will also not be able to bypass the Oberammergau Passion Play

Theatre without browsing in the fascinating documentation of the production staged here, documentation that captures the vitality of the centuries-old heritage. The reason for the origin of the play was a collective catastrophe, a plague epidemic in the Thirty Years' War. Precisely why it was that death was combatted by means of a passion play, is the question placed by Oberammergau.

What about encounters with the local people – can they too become significant stations for the meditating wanderer? Although paradise may not be on the banks of the Ammer, there is a good chance that you will meet friendly, warm people who are able and keen to communicate. And as these characteristics are as widespread as they are, it is easy to speculate that they must be the result of long-term nurturing across generations, similar to a well-maintained English lawn that represents the successful work of more than one generation. Anyone in search of forces that have been at work on a long-term basis will find them in the Augustinian Canons in Rottenbuch.

From the 12th century on, when the Welfs tasked them with pastoral care in Ammer Valley, up to secularisation in 1803 they shaped the spirituality of the people of the region. Typically, almost all churches in the parishes they looked after, feature the central symbol of this fellowship and their founding father in a prominent place: the burning heart.

This symbol too, is worth appropriating for meditative purposes! At first glance it seems to signify no more than the German gingerbread heart an Oktoberfest visitor may bestow upon his girlfriend: I like you; I miss you; I want to be with you – a relationship symbol or an erotic symbol, so to speak, the symbol that forms the focus of the French "Book of the smitten heart" in the late Middle Ages, for example.

Talk of the heart originates from much earlier, though. Even in early oriental testimonies it bore the psychological meaning of man's centre, the root of all feelings, needs, judgements and actions, analogous to its central physiological function as one of the body's organs. According to extracts from the Old Testament, the heart can be hardened, stubborn, darkened, or it can be an organ attuned to perception, while at the same time being a source of kindness and loving care. This was particularly the case if "the heart of stone" was taken from man to be replaced by a "heart of flesh", as was the case in Ezekiel. The heart provides a base for secret communication among people – as in the God/man relationship – that can go as far as becoming the dwelling of the other.

In the words of a love song: "You are in my heart". And if the other is missing, the heart is filled with longing; if the other is present, the heart experiences feelings of transformation, ensoulment and enlivenment.

It is surprising, however, that the image of the heart is associated with an image of fire. Perhaps this can be explained simply in that a sensation of burning can be felt in the chest when experiencing certain emotions, be it happiness or hurt. And this is most probably based on a feeling of cold when experiencing rejection and a feeling of warmth when experiencing loving care. This logic is then applied to increased love energy, namely in the form of a flame – fire. Added to that, life in today's society, whose coldness is lamented by literature with numerous images illustrating large-scale glaciation, it may be possible to understand why the church has always been praying to God to "ignite the fire of His love" in man.

These connections are particularly apparent in the figure of fire-headed Augustinus, the passionate admirer of God and man, who also denotes the expression: "What you wish to ignite in others must burn within yourself." The fact that he has justifiably been given the burning heart as a symbol is confirmed by his theory of the heart's natural talent to love: "Besides truth, man has an internal secret ability to love, which, like a weight, draws him away from himself toward others, and in particular toward the most supreme. The weight of love is what gives man his social qualities."

So, if the burning heart symbol accompanies the hiker in the Ammergau Alps as a route marker, should the meditative walker yearn for some of the sparks from the Augustinian fire to glow or shine in him too, that is to say, that the benefit of hiking should manifest itself as an increase in love energy? An answer to this question may presuppose that a distinction is made between the different traditions of meditation. While the eastern tradition tends to show in a direction of "dimming" the impetus of the heart and of ridding oneself of this impetus, the tendency of meditation as we have known it in our cultural sphere in the last two thousand years is towards personalising all energies, channelling them in terms of polar, dialogical tension between the I and another person. The impact can by all means be an increased love of life and happiness. If we look at the burning hearts of the light-hearted Oberammergau inhabitants in the high altarpiece in the parish church, these are floating – on a tray carried by angels – in the direction of the skies towards the "heavenly mother", who is smilingly glancing down, and her son. This illustration of the liturgical

On the Altherrenweg at Unterammergau

"Sursum corda!" – "Lift up your hearts!" to some degree simulates the boisterous gesture of the lad tossing his hat up into the air, and also slightly resembles the generous "tossing of the heart across the ditch" as is the case in Ella Fitzgerald's "Baby, take all of me". A wanderer blessed with a spirit of this nature could happily stride along just like his Eichendorff ancestors did, imagining or singing the song: "When God wishes to show true favour to someone / he sends him out into the wide world / and points out his miracles / in mountain and wood and river and field."

Whether the true hiking guest would find this mental image appealing is really a question of style and musicality. In any event, one would wish upon him that his journey off the beaten track – in moments of silence, away from all acoustic pollution and where global noises become silent – results in a fine tuning of his audible senses, allowing him to hear the beating of his heart.

The 15 stations

1 Pilgrimage Church of Wies (Wieskirche)

Steeped in history

When standing in the centre of the Pilgrimage Church of Wies and looking up at the fresco in the main dome by Baptist Johann Zimmermann, our gaze is literally drawn to the large gate. It is the "gate to eternity", and undoubtedly epitomises one of the most important Christian messages in Wies theology.

The gate to paradise is still closed. The ancient God of time Chronos is lying on the ground; he is no longer holding the hour glass and the scythe. The angel's book is still closed. The snake above it has been transformed into a ring, the symbol for eternity, without a beginning or an end. And at the very top of the gate we can see the words: "Tempus non erit amplius", which means "Time shall be no more".

Absorbed

When glancing at the door a little longer, the cross in its centre becomes increasingly more apparent. Directly in the centre of the cross is the keyhole. That is, at the exact same location as the heart of crucified Christ. We could formulate the message in this as follows: Jesus' heart, his love, is the key to the afterlife, to paradise.

It wants to communicate to us: We need not fear the moment of crossing the threshold. At that point man need no longer hope, he can trust and follow his longings.

Internalised

"Time shall be no more" also aims to communicate: Man's goal is the moment in which there is no more past, no future and perhaps also no more present. Everything is thus about the current moment, the now. It also wants to inform us: We are already in eternity today, in heavenly Jerusalem, in heaven on earth. Here and now.

Let us take a quiet moment, pause and ask ourselves: What am I doing with my time? How strongly am I affected by experiences from my past? How much strength and energy am I wasting in worrying about the future?

Those who succeed at being in the moment, have conquered paradise.

The gate to eternity in the Pilgrimage Church of Wies

2 Rottenbuch Abbey (Kloster Rottenbuch)

Steeped in history

Rottenbuch Abbey was built in 1073. Raitenpuech, a cleared strip of land that housed hermits as far back as 1070 and before, was a generous gift from the Duke of Bavaria Welf I and his wife Judith, who lived in the Welfenburg Castle in nearby Peiting.

The abbey was handed to the new order of the Augustinian Canon. As a reform abbey, Rottenbuch supported the church reform of Pope Gregor VII and as such achieved its golden age as early as the beginning of the 12th century.

It is assumed that the Roman collegiate church was erected in honour of the Virgin Mother between 1085 and 1125. Over the centuries the church was first renovated in the Gothic style, and later, in the 18th century, converted to Baroque by Joseph Schmuzer and his son Franz Xaver.

Absorbed

In the Middle Ages, monasterys were not only spiritual and religious central points, but also an essential part of the temporal society. For the most part, these were in the service of the King, and at the same time feudal lords for the farmers. Besides pastoral care, they looked after the ill, provided accommodation for travellers and acted as money lenders. They engaged in handicrafts, farming, trade and often even ran monastic schools. They cultivated herbs and their dispensaries became centres for healing arts. Only in the late Middle Ages were some of these tasks assumed by the newly founded cities.

The communal life in monasterial societies was defined by the monks' rules. The oldest occidental observance is that of Saint Augustinus. The canons of Rottenbuch also lived in accordance with this observance. Augustinus is one of four church fathers, and is mostly depicted with the attribute of the burning heart.

Internalised

"Nobody may focus on his own benefits while working, rather all work shall be performed in the service of the community, and this shall occur with more diligence and enthusiasm than would be the case were each to work on his own and for his own needs. After all, it is written about love that it seeks not its own benefit, meaning: it places the interests of the community above self-interest and not vice versa. The fact that I place more emphasis on concerning myself with the communal interests than your own is thus a touchstone for your progress. And as such, all man's past distresses shall leave something that is lasting and superior, namely love."

Extract from Augustinus' observance (V/2)

The parish (former collegiate) church of Rottenbuch

3 Lake Soier (Soier See)

Steeped in history

Bad Bayersoien owes its name to two lakes that developed during the last Ice Age. The name is derived from the Celts who lived here once upon a time. The Celtic name for the site was "Seun", which means "at the lakes". It was only from the 19th century onwards that the full name Bayersoien was passed on to us.

The so-called upper lake was drained in 1803 for purposes of litter harvesting. The lower lake we see today is typical of this high moor landscape. It is cleaned from time to time, and maintained as a relaxation oasis for the people living here and their guests. At the same time the high moor landscape around the lake is allowed to develop naturally in the interests of nature conservation.

Absorbed

Why are lakes so fascinating? Lakes provide an atmosphere of calmness, security, vastness and depth. This results in a connection with our feelings. A lake also bears a touch of secrecy – it reaches deep areas within us, namely our soul. The German words "See" and "Seele" are related: "Seele" (soul) is derived from Old German and means "belonging to the 'See' (lake)"; our forefathers deemed lakes to be places where the souls of the unborn and the dead lived. So even our forefathers did not consider our souls to be exclusively linked to the body.

Sine aqua non vita: Water and life are directly linked. If seen in this way, one could say: Our soul yearns for the lake.

Internalised

Let us take some time, sit at the lake and get in touch with our soul. Lama Govinda said in this regard: "Oblivious of everything you are able to recognise the principle of the inner centre. Since those who are unable to find eternity in their own hearts, shall not find outside what he did not create inside. After all, the world is merely a mirror of what is in our own being; imperfect it appears to the incomplete mind."

Lake Soier

4 Scheibum

Steeped in history

The source of the river Ammer is in Graswang Valley. It drains a part of the Ammer Mountain Range, flows into the Lake Ammer north of Weilheim and is called the river Amper when it meets the river Isar in Moosburg. The Ammer Valley is one of the most beautiful natural river valleys in the northern Limestone Alps. The entire river is 185 km long.

During the Wurm Ice Age, around 120,000 years ago, the Ammer meandered its way through the Ammer-Loisach uplands after leaving the Alps. The splendid Ammer Gorge (Ammerschlucht) between Altenau and Peißenberg was formed in this manner. Here, approximately 15 km from its source, the Ammer created this impressive gap in the rock, the Scheibum, which measures 600 m in length, is up to 80 m deep and has been under protection since as early as 1949.

Absorbed

How was it possible for this magnificent natural structure to develop? We can assume that the rock gate of the Scheibum was formed by a meander that encountered a meander core. It is highly likely that this is the reason for its name: "Scheib-um", "Scheibe" being a disc, therefore "rotating disc". We can visualise this as a turning water disk that cannot find an exit, that is, it keeps on spinning. Over the centuries, the water dug deeper and deeper into the rock. This finally resulted in a narrow gap, which the river Ammer could then use to continue its superb piece of work.

The Scheibum consists of marl and sandstone. The various rock layers that occurred during the opening of the Alpine folds around 25 – 30 million years ago can be clearly seen here in the form of natural limestone, loam, white and grey quartz as well as slate.

Internalised

"There is nothing in the world that is softer and more yielding than water. And yet, the manner in which it overcomes the rigid cannot be equalled by any other. Nothing is able to change it. The fact that the weak will overcome the strong, and that which is yielding will overcome the rigid is known to everyone on earth, but no one is able to act accordingly."
Laotse (Chinese philosopher, 6 BC)

Nature invites us to learn from it. What personal weaknesses am I aware of that I can transform into strengths? Which of these assumed weaknesses are already actually personal strengths?

The Ammer Gorge at the Scheibum

5 Fatima Chapel (Fatimakapelle)

Steeped in history

Josef Leismiller from the town of Saulgrub was one of many of his generation to have experienced the same fate: As a young man, he had to go to Russia in 1939 for the Second World War. However, his path of suffering did not end when the war ended. He spent five years at the Minsk prisoner-of-war camp, in which tens of thousands of young men starved to death at the time.

During this time of great fear, Josef Leismiller vowed to build a chapel if ever he should return home. He returned to Saulgrub in 1949. Four years later he began his journey to Fatima, the Portuguese place of pilgrimage. He brought back a statue of the Holy Virgin of Fatima. On his return, he started building the Fatima Chapel together with a friend, a bricklayer. The chapel was consecrated on 12 September 1954.

Absorbed

Chapels such as these are also known as votive chapels. "Votive" is derived from the Latin word "votum", meaning a vow. The religious custom of making a vow dates back as early as the Stone Age. The Gods were presented supplications and offerings of thanks at holy places.

The votive cult has also been known since the beginning of Christian tradition. This custom is particularly noticeable in pilgrimage churches or chapels, where votive paintings, votive candles or votive sculptures such as the famous sculptures of babies (Fatschenkinder) are a common occurrence.

We know votive trees from nature, and votive churches or votive chapels as examples of architecture. The reason for presenting a votive offering to a Saint was more often than not an appeal or thanks for deliverance from a crisis, such as an illness, a catastrophe or some other desperate situation.

Internalised

"He who reflects on his life with thanks shall agree with that, which he has experienced. He shall no longer rebel against himself or his fate. He shall recognise that everyday anew an angel enters his life to protect him from misery and to impart on him his loving and healing closeness."

Extract from "Der Engel der Dankbarkeit" (The Angel of Thanks), by: Anselm Grün, 50 Engel für das Jahr (50 Angels for the Year), HERDER spektrum Bd. 4902, p. 43 © Verlag Herder GmbH, Freiburg im Breisgau, 34th edition 2008

The word "thank" is derived from "think". It invites us to think about our own thankfulness. What demands do I have of life? Are there people for whom I am thankful? What wounds and injuries can I accept with thanks?

The Fatima Chapel at Saulgrub

6 Rochusfeld

Steeped in history

Here in Rochusfeld near Bad Kohlgrub we come across a typical high moor landscape of the foothills of the Alps. This landscape developed after the last Ice Age more than 10,000 years ago. After melting, the glaciers left behind small lakes that had neither tributaries nor runoffs and no connection to the ground water. During the course of the following centuries drastic, changing climatic conditions took place again and again.

Times of extreme heat followed by extremely cold periods; from extreme droughts to flooding. Plants in oxygen-deprived and acid water did not rot, rather they turned to peat. This is how the low moor developed. Moss, grass, shrubs and trees spread out from the shores. The lakes eventually silted up and the moor grew ever higher, layer by layer. And the result is this unique landscape, the mountain pine moor of the foothills of the Alps, shaped by nature.

Absorbed

Man has made use of the moor from time immemorial. In the early days special tools were used to dig up the peat, which was dried over long periods and then used for heating. The heating value was comparable with that of brown coal. Since discovering its healing effects in 1870, the Kohlgrubers used their valuable moor increasingly more as a medium for curing ailments. In this manner, nature's power was used to promote health in humans.

When swimming in a warm, thick moor the body absorbs everything that has been conserved in the moor over thousands of years: the sun's light, the earth's power and the energy of the healing agents of millions of plants. The moor's holistic healing power enhances stimulation of the metabolism and circulation, acts as a hormone regulator, promotes the immune system and provides deep relaxation.

Internalised

Let us be inspired by nature around us. Let us appreciate the century-old healing power surrounding us.

I walk a few steps on this healing earth. I walk on it with mindfulness and awareness of nature's ancient wisdom. My inner image of Mother Earth assists me in this. She feeds me, protects me, carries me and heals me. I may accept everything with gratitude.

Moor soil

7

Kappel Church (Kappelkirche)

Steeped in history

The location of the Kappel church is the oldest place of prayer in upper Ammer Valley. As far back as 900, Eticho from the House of Welf is believed to have settled here as a hermit. Later on, it is believed, a monastery was even erected here.

In the 15th century, the Kappel church became the goal of pilgrims, who came here to honour the Relic of the Holy Blood. This relic is associated with a legend, according to which the blind Roman soldier Longinus, who pierced the side of Jesus with a spear, is said to have mixed the blood of the crucified Christ with earth and applied this to his eyes. The legend further relates that he was able to see again after this. In ecclesiastical circles he is considered the first heathen confessor to Christianity.

Absorbed

Places of grace or pilgrimage such as the Kappel have always been the goal of people seeking healing. Observing and touching relics, or even just being close to them, gave them hope to be able to share in the divine message of salvation.

Salvation of body and soul means becoming "whole", in the sense of: becoming the whole person my creator intended me to be in the depth of my soul. The legend of the soldier who regained his sight wants to bring home that people can change. When the moment is right, our eyes open and our vision becomes clear. We see things in a different perspective than previously.

Internalised

We are invited to pause, close our eyes and to ponder the following thoughts: Do I also know of situations in my life, in which my eyes suddenly opened? Do I find it difficult to change my way of seeing others? Am I able to withdraw from the judgement of others?

"Seeing more clearly" also clears my thoughts, my words and my judgements. To have my own way of seeing makes me free and independent of the evaluations of others.

The Kappel Church at Unterammergau

8 Hörnle

Steeped in history

Between the foothills of the Alps and the Alpine Mountain Range, the Hörnle dominates the view to the south. Strictly speaking, we are referring to the Hörnle-group with its three tips, of which the "Hintere Hörnle" is the highest with a peak of 1548 m.

In contrast to the rugged limestone peaks of the Laber, Ettaler Manndl and Klammspitzkamm, the Hörnle peaks are more round and tree-covered. This is particularly due to the flysch, which is relatively unstable. The limestone layer beneath this causes the surface water to dam up, which explains why the moistest ground conditions are found here in the Ammergau Alps.

Absorbed

The Hörnle is a popular hiking destination, thanks to the amazing views it offers. The north reveals a panoramic view of the Bavarian Alpine foothills to hikers. Starting in the west, they are treated to a view of the Auerberg then the Hohenpeißenberg, the Lake Ammer, then the Lake Starnberg and finally the Benediktenwand. Weather permitting, it is even possible to see the state capital Munich and the peaks of the Bavarian Forest.

In the southern direction the breathtaking panoramic view spreads across the entire mountain chain of the Limestone Alps. Our view begins at the eastern tops of the Karwendel Mountains, followed by the Wettersteingroup and Germany's highest mountain, the Zugspitze, and finally the Allgäu Mountains and the Lech Valley in the south-west.

"... and God made the firmament, and divided the waters which were under the firmament from the waters which were above the firmament: And it was so. And God called the firmament Heaven. And the evening and the morning were the second day. And God said: Let the waters unter the heaven be gathered onto one place..."
King James Bible, V 1769, Genesis 1

These words from the history of creation reinforce our feelings up here on the peak. It is more than satisfaction, it is a feeling of freedom and endless expanse. All cultures have holy mountains; they are always surrounded by peacefulness. Peacefulness that comes from the outside allows me to become peaceful on the inside. It also provides my heart with peacefulness. When I close my eyes and allow myself to focus on my heart I can clearly feel my heart beating. I can gradually feel how my heart begins to beat slower and slower and how the peacefulness spreads throughout my whole body.

View from the Hoernle of Unterammergau and the Ammer Mountains

9 Passion Play Theatre (Passionstheater)

Steeped in history

During the Thirty Years' War, the plague also reached Oberammergau in 1632. After 84 people had lost their lives to the desease, the village inhabitants vowed in 1633 to perform a play of the suffering and death of Jesus Christ every ten years. It is said that no single person died after this solemn vow was taken.

In Whitsun 1634 the stage was set up at the village cemetery for the first play. Almost 200 years later the event was relocated, to the passion field. In the years that followed, the wooden stage was extended with props and stage technology. The spectator area was initially provisionally furnished with wood, to be replaced by stone later on. In 1929 the theatre was revamped to the state we see it today, and in 2008 a mobile roof construction made of steel and synthetic material was added to the stage.

Absorbed

The mystery play with the theme of the suffering and death of Christ was already performed in Germany as far back as 1330. It was initially only performed on Good Friday. Passion plays in later years comprised the entire Christian salvific history of the Old and New Testaments. From the 15th century onwards, this principal type of mediaeval religious play lasted two to three days, and often included several thousand participants.

Passion plays were promoted by the Catholic reform movement, and as such experienced their prime during the 16th and 18th century. In those days more than 250 passion play locations developed in the Bavarian and Austrian regions. The performers of these plays were the inhabitants, who took part as an exercise of experiencing the suffering, death and resurrection of Jesus Christ.

Internalised

In the German language we equate the word "Passion" with "Leidenschaft". The term is ambiguous for the following reason: "Leidenschaft" derives from "leiden", which originally meant "to set forth", "to travel to foreign lands". And those who travelled a great deal had many experiences and often had to endure great hardships in those days. Thus the word changed its meaning to describe something like "suffer pains".

Passion in the Christian message stands for the crucifixion and the resurrection, that is, redemption.

To live with passion thus means to live humbly and to accept life's hard and painful experiences. However, we also live our passion in our feelings, our exaltation and our devotion.

The Oberammergau Passion Play 2000, tableau "Departure of Tobias"

0 Monument of Crucifixion (Kreuzigungsgruppe)

Steeped in history

In 1871, the people of Oberammergau organised a special production of the passion plays in honour of King Ludwig II. He was so enthused by the performance that he bestowed upon the town this marble Monument of Crucifixion as a token of his thanks. It displays the crucifixion scene with Mother Mary and the disciple Johannes. Munich-born Johann von Halbig was the sculptor.

The King himself decided on this location, as the approaching visitors could see it perfectly from all sides. The monument was visible from almost all the houses in the village, and from up here the view over the whole of the Ammer Valley was marvellous. The King had also hoped that this gently rising hill would one day be the endpoint of a Mount Calvary. The inauguration took place on 15 October 1875 here at the Osterbichl in the presence of His Majesty.

Absorbed

The depiction of Christ on the cross has been a central theme of Christian art since the Romanesque period. The manner in which this is displayed has however changed over the centuries. Up until around 1250 (end of Romanesque period) Jesus was primarily depicted as Christ the King: spirited, dignified, bearing the royal crown, legs next to each other. He has conquered death and is returning in the glory.

In an attempt to anthropomorphise the divine in the Gothic period, artists increasingly also emphasised the suffering. Christ on the cross is often depicted as dead or in the process of dying. His feet are crossed, the royal crown has become a crown of thorns, the facial expression is increasingly painful.

Internalised

The cross is as old as humankind. It initially symbolised the earthly, like the four seasons or the four points of the compass. Later, as a wheel cross it signified the light and the sun. In Christianity the cross became the symbol for the death of Jesus, but also for his resurrection and his redemption.

In everyday life the cross represents our worries, the burden of life and also backache. It represents the decision as to which path we should take, and encounters with other people, as well as communicating and bringing together.

This opens the following beautiful vision to me: I take the cross to be the symbol that invites me to gather myself in its centre. This enables me to reorientate myself, to open up and then to confidently proceed along my path.

Monument of Crucifixion at Oberammergau

11 Döttenbichl

Steeped in history

Archaeological finds in Döttenbichl indicate that Roman legions had advanced as far as this via the Alps as long ago as 15 BC, the era of Emperor Augustus. At these times, people had already been living in the Alpine region for around 10,000 years. A large number of weapons, in particular arrow tips and projectiles, discovered here lead us to believe that the Romans and the Celts living in the region at the time engaged in a warlike conflict.

Among other things, the place name Oberammergau is an indicator of Celtic habitation. It is said to derive from the Celtic name "Ambrigo", which in turn comes from the Celtic designation for a river, "Ambara" or "Ampra". This would also explain the name Ammer, known as Amper until the 14th century, and which is still the case between the Lake Ammer and where it meets the river Isar.

Absorbed

The finds clearly indicate that the Döttenbichl at Oberammergau was a cult site from the late Ice Age and the early Roman period onwards. Celtic cult sites are mostly found on elevated landscape formations such as hilltops or hills. For our forefathers these sites were sacred places where they communicated with their godheads. They used altars to scarifice animals, beverages and food to the godheads in the rising smoke of the flames.

The most important Celtic celebrations took place at very particular times in the wheel of the year. These were social ceremonies and compulsory events. The main festivals were Samhain (turn of the year 31 October/ 1 November), Imbolc (light and cleaning festival 31 January/ 1 February), Beltane (festival of fertility 30 April/ 1 May) and Lugnasad (harvesting preparation 31 July/ 1 August).

"Every part of this country is sacred to my people. Every hill-side, every valley, every plain and grove has been hallowed by some fond memory or some sad experience of my tribe. Even the rocks that seem to lie dumb as they swelter in the sun along the silent seashore in solemn grandeur thrill with memories of past events connected with the fate of my people, and the very dust under your feet responds more lovingly to our footsteps than to yours, because it is the ashes of our ancestors, and our bare feet are conscious of the sympathetic touch, for the soil is rich with the life of our kindred."

Chief Seattle (Duwamish Indian, North America)

How do I see my ancestors, my parents today? Do I value their wisdom? Is my life rooted? Are there people, traditions and places in my life that provide me with support and strength?

Water basin at the Grottenweg (19th century)

2 Ettal Abbey (Kloster Ettal)

Steeped in history

The massive dome of the Ettal abbey rises to the heavens like a temple. After an angel had appeared to him, Emperor Ludwig the Bavarian endowed this cloister here in the narrow bottom of the valley with a height of almost 900 m. He named it "frawen ê-tal", which we translate as "the honourable valley of our lady".

The Gothic central structure with twelve corners and the location here in the valley were just as unusual as the abbey's form of organisation. In addition to the monks and their abbots, knights, their wives and their masters also lived here. However, the knights' monastery was closed again in the 14th century.

In the early part of the 18th century the founding idea was again taken up and a knight academy was set up in the abbey. It served primarily as a place of training for aristocratic students that came from all over the then Holy Roman Empire.

Absorbed

We do not have any proof, but it is certainly conceivable that the then popular legend of King Arthur and the Knights of the Holy Grail may have played a role when the abbey was designed.

King Ludwig II. wrote the following lines to Richard Wagner: "In the distance at the end of the valley, the Church of Ettal rises from the dark pine green. Emperor Ludwig the Bavarian is believed to have built this church according to the plan of Mont Salvat's Grail temple ..." He is referring to Wolfram von Eschenbach's legend "Parsifal", a knight of King Arthur's Round Table who found the Holy Grail after an extended period of wandering.

Internalised

Let us allow ourselves to experience the whole dimension of this imposing monastery complex from this raised location. We are invited to feel the wonderful magic of this holy place.

What do I find special in this location? What feelings does it trigger in me? Did the builders of this abbey manage to blend it with the unique landscape created by nature almost 700 years ago?

View of Ettal from the Meditation Trail

3 Ammer springs (Ammerquellen)

Steeped in history

To the west of Graswang the headstreams of the Linder seep away in the permeable, limey underground of the Neualmgrieß and the Lindergrieß. Here in Weidmoos, 850 m above sea level, they reappear as rising, bubbling water holes, so-called plunge pools. We are looking at the little Ammer springs (Kleine Ammerquellen). It does not take long before the spring-fed pools turn into two little streams, which then soon unite to form the little river Ammer. This little river Ammer loops and winds its way over the low moor ground of the Ettal basin. From the wide stream bed of the large river Ammer (Große Ammer) it then flows in a northerly direction.

The young moraine landscape that developed in Wurm Ice Age causes the Ammer to cut into the molasses banks to a depth of up to 80 m. The impressive Ammer gorge ends in Peißenberg. Not far from Dießen, the river flows into the Lake Ammer, which it leaves as the Amper and subsequently joins the river Isar near Moosburg.

Absorbed

Because of the ingress of cold air in the region of the Bavarian Alps and due to a single autumn haymaking, it was possible for a unique vegetation to survive in this low moor. For example, the rare wild flower "Karlszepter" blossoms more profusely here in the Weidmoos (peat bog) than anywhere else in Bavaria.

The rampant growth of the so-called "Armleuchteralgen" (chandelier algae) in the fast-flowing spring-fed streams is proof of the extremely high water quality. Those algae are normally only found in still waters. The extensive valley floor moors of the Ettal Weidmoos are among the internationally most significant moors in Bavaria.

Internalised

Springs always have a positive effect on their surroundings; they add magic to the place where they rise. The bubbling life force of the water has a stimulating, inspiring and harmonising effect.

Springs counted as sanctuaries to our ancestors, and were also often central points for religious and social life in Christianity.

Springs are places of strength and healing – they are the origin of new life.

We are invited to try the following exercise: I breathe in through my nose and out through my mouth, which is slightly open in my thoughts. I follow the inhaled spring water which starts flowing from my crown to my soles, cleansing me in the process.

Springs of the Ammer

4 Gertrudis Chapel (Gertrudiskapelle)

Steeped in history

The Dickelschwaig chapel was built by the monks of the Ettal abbey in 1694. The hexagonal central structure features a massive Baroque onion dome. The crest and inscription of then Abbot Romaldus Haimblinger (RHAZE) of Ettal can be seen above the portal.

The art on the interior of the church is by Jakob Zeiller from the year 1755, the same artist who also created the spectacular dome fresco in the Ettal abbey. In the early days the Gertrudis Chapel was frequently the destination for pilgrimages by the Ettal townsmen. Today, every year on the Day of the Patron Saint Hubertus mass is read for all forestry employees.

Absorbed

The chapel was consecrated to Gertrud von Helfta, who was extremely popular at the time of its construction (memorial day 17 November). Gertrud, also known as the Great, lived in the second half of the 13th century and was an important advocate of female mysticism. She was an exceptionally well-educated woman. She had visions of encounters with Jesus and mystic experiences that resulted in her strong love towards Jesus. Although she was so spiritual she did not live a secluded life.

Her love for people was as strong as the love she felt for Jesus, which made her a sought-after adviser and pastor. She translated parts of the Holy Scripture and left the descriptions of her visions, meditations and her religious knowledge to posterity.

The symbol for her immense love to Jesus is the burning heart.

We are invited to pause and to focus our attention towards the middle of our chest, the area of the spiritual heart. We continue breathing slowly and imagine a small warm light at our heart.

Each time we breathe in we connect deeper with the glow in our body. We allow healing light to flow into us. And we hear the meditative words of Saint Gertrud:

"The wonderful effect of the light flows through my body, it enters my most inner core; it seems to dissolve all barriers and I feel as though my body and my soul were nothing but light, godly light."
(Gertrud von Helfta)

The Chapel of Gertrudis and the forester's lodge Dickelschwaig

5 Linderhof Palace (Schloss Linderhof)

Steeped in history

"An eternal mystery to myself and to others is what I wish to be", wrote King Ludwig II. in a letter to his governess Sybille Meilhaus, and in another: "Building, as well as gripping reading matter and occasionally the theatre, always induces the most wonderful enjoyment."

After his first meeting with the king, Richard Wagner said: "Unfortunately he is so pleasant and spirited, soulful and blissful that I fear his life may fade away like a fleeting god's dream in this mean world."

Ludwig himself called his castles and structures "... poetic retreats where one can forget the dreadful time in which we live for some time." And of the Gurnemanz' retreat in the third act of the opera "Parsifal" he said "... there, on the sacred site I can already hear the ominous silver trombones from the Castle of the Grail ..."

Absorbed

Preserved quotes and letters of the king and statements about him enable us to imagine the types of conflict he experienced and how he tried to escape from them. He became King of Bavaria at the tender age of 18. Very early on in his reign he was involved in disastrous wars.

In his yearning for redemption Ludwig escaped into the vision of a better world. He created a counterworld for himself and identified more and more with Parsifal, the knight of the legendary King Arthur of the Round Table from the 12th century world of legends. The Grail theme in Richard Wagner's last work is a good description of the secret history of his soul.

Let us take a moment and try and imagine the emotional life of this man plagued by conflicts. Unaffected by the numerous interpretations and assumptions made about the king's emotional life and state of mind, we can ask ourselves the following question: Am I also aware of situations in my life, in which my tasks became constraints? What are my visions and dreams, and how am I living them? Are there values that I might like to fight for? How do I deal with conflicts?

The Water Parterre with the Temple of Venus

Directions

Directions

The following route description will provide you with pointers. It does not replace a hiking map or independent orientation in the area.

Pilgrimage Church of Wies (Wieskirche) 1

After the pilgrimage to the Scourged Saviour in Wies took on increasingly new dimensions Steingaden Abbey decided to build a large pilgrimage church. Between 1745 and 1754 one of the most beautiful Rococo churches in southern Germany was erected within an extremely short period of time.

The Pilgrimage Church of Wies combines centrally planned building typical for the Renaissance with Roman basilica style. The choir ambulatory is very characteristic of large pilgrimage churches of the Middle Ages. The Pilgrimage Church of Wies manages to interpret the attitude towards life in those bygone times as no other church does. It is frequently also referred to as a spatial wonder, an architecture of light that emits depth, lightness, harmony and happiness. The accomplished Rococo art by Dominikus and Johann Baptist Zimmermann has no doubt contributed to the fact that the Pilgrimage Church of Wies has been recognised as a world heritage site by UNESCO.

Our walk starts at the portal of the Pilgrimage Church of Wies and we proceed along the path in the direction of the parking area, located slightly below the church. Next to the small chapel at the bottom, we turn right and continue along the road.

Pilgrimage Chapel of the Scourged Saviour (Wallfahrtskapelle zum Gegeißelten Heiland)

A pilgrimage, accompanied by many prayers, developed soon after the Miracle of Tears of 14 June 1738. Thereupon this chapel was built in 1740, but within a short period of time was found to be too small.

The small blue signs with the symbolic shells indicate that we are following a stretch of road that is running in the opposite direction to the Way of St. James. This part of the

The Pilgrimage Church of Wies

famous pilgrimage path starts in Munich and leads to the Lake Constance, finally ending in Santiago de Compostela in Spain.

We turn right into the road, travel a short distance on a narrow tarred stretch until a curve to the right appears. We leave the road at this point and follow a path to the left that leads through a row of trees across the meadows to an adult education college. Here we first turn to the right, leave the tarred road after the seminar centre's buildings, again in a curve to the right, and take the road to the left into the forest. We follow the forestry road and ignore various roads entering from the left. The Schwarzenbach flows parallel to our road on the right, winding its natural course through dense undergrowth. At the point where the stream can be crossed, we leave the path to the right in an easterly direction and cross a small flat area.

Our path leads up into a small wood. After the short rise, we keep to the right at the fork. From here, we have a wonderful view over the Ammergau Mountains – the Hohe Bleick can be seen to the right, and opposite us the first houses of Wildsteig can already be seen on the hill.

Our path continues through moor-like meadows. After crossing a stream we reach a path that we first follow for a short while to the left. Soon after, we turn to the right up the hill to the Holz district. We pass a few

Field crucifix in the Ammer Mountains

agricultural estates and then reach a small chapel, located to the left of the path.

This trinity chapel is usually open, and it is worth taking a short rest here.

Trinity Chapel (Dreifaltigkeitskapelle)

The Trinity Chapel was built in1970. Its ceiling fresco shows a representation of the trinity and the crowning of Mary in the presence of the saintly Mother Anna and Saint Joseph.

We continue on our path and reach a crossing, where we read *"Pilgerweg"* on the street sign opposite, and continue to the left. On the hill in front of us we reach the town hall on the left hand side. *Kirchstraße* on the opposite side of the street brings us into the centre of Wildsteig. Shortly before the school building we turn to the left down to the Church of St. Jacob.

Church of St. Jacob (Jakobskirche)

According to documents, a church of Saint Margareta in Wildsteig was first mentioned in 1477. The current building derives from the beginning of the 18th century, and at the latest since this time Saint Jacob the Elder has been the patron. This is a simple roofed hall with fine stucco work that unifies elements of the end of the Rococo style with classicism. One of the church's oldest art works is the altarpiece, which depicts both patrons of the church, the saints Margareta and Jacob, kneeling before the Infant Jesus.

Leaving the church, we take the footpath to the left down the hill and pass the Lourdes Grotto dating from 1908 – one of the most significant grotto systems in southern Germany. We cross the Dorfbach and reach the other side of the street. At the fork up ahead of us, we first remain to the left and then leave the town by continuing straight on. A subway brings us to the other side of the town bypass. Soon thereafter, we orient ourselves to the right and continue walking approx. 1 km on the left of the main road.

About halfway along this stretch, the path steps descend past a parking place for hikers and our way continues on a narrow path. We leave the traffic noise once again on a gently climbing agricultural road. We remain on this path until we reach a small wood, which we cross downhill.

On the meadow path, after a bridge, we pass a farmstead to the left. We then take the next fork to the right onto the climbing tarred road. Behind the next property we continue to the left and soon see the first houses of Rottenbuch.

We follow the road into the town and proceed along *Weihanger* to the main road. We cross over using the pedestrian bridge and continue to the left.

The monument to Saint Leonhard reminds us of the traditional Rottenbuch horse procession, which takes place in late autumn every year. We continue on the opposite side of the street, passing the old cloister gate, and find ourselves in the Rottenbuch cloister yard. A few steps later, we arrive at the church tower and the portal of the original collegiate church.

Rottenbuch Abbey (Kloster Rottenbuch) Birth of Mary Parish Church (former collegiate church) 2

Construction of the collegiate church started in 1085. The three-aisled Romanic basilica with transept was completed in 1125. During the 15th century, the three-aisled chancel was first torn down and rebuilt as a single aisle. Thereafter, the transept and nave were rebuilt in the late Gothic style. In the 18th century the interior was converted to the Rococo style.

After the collapse of the old belfry, a freestanding tower was constructed in 1439 and acquired a classicist spire in 1780/81.

Detour to Frauenbrünnerl Chapel:
Before passing the archway, we turn to the right into *Franz-von-Heeren-Straße*. After approx. 150 m we follow a footpath to the left, which leads through a small wood to the main road in the direction of Böbing, and takes us down the valley to the right, directly to the chapel.

Frauenbrünnerl Chapel

The octagonal chapel is a favourite place of meditation, and was built over a spring in 1688. This was originally a Gothic wayside shrine with a much-revered Madonna. This Gothic miraculous image dating from the 15th century can today be admired in the high altar of 1705.

We leave the cloister yard through an archway in a north-westerly direction. After approx. 50 m we turn right onto the road before the district sewage works and proceed alongside the old cloister wall. Our path winds through a mixed woodland, accompanied by small bubbling streams, down to the Ammer.

picture on the right: Dome fresco in the parish church of Rottenbuch

Regu
la

Lake Soier with view of Bad Bayersoien

We continue a short while along the river bank, cross the main road to the right before the bridge and walk along the tarred road through the parking area of the old Ammer Mill, which today houses a clinic.

Ammer Mill (Ammermühle)

This contained the cloister's sawmill and a grain mill. The names of the operators have been documented since around 1500. It is assumed that in 1641 floodwaters destroyed the Ammer mill, although the reconstruction took place shortly afterwards. The milling operation ceased in 1902. The sawing operation continued functioning until 1962. Today the historic building houses a spa clinic.

At the end of the park, we cross the Ammer and soon reach a path that rises gently at first to the next wooded area. We continue straight on, and our path becomes gradually steeper until we reach a road that makes a broad curve. We follow this gently uphill to the right until we leave the wood once again behind the next curve to the left.

Our view increases again, we climb even higher, and see the first houses of Schönberg in front of us. Before these, we reach a crossroads, where we continue straight on along a path of concrete slabs. At the next road, we turn to the left up a gentle climbing, turn right at the top and then reach the Assumption of Mary parish church of Schönberg.

The thoroughfare proceeds downhill again, and after passing a children's playground on the right hand side it turns to the left. In the curve to the left, we turn right into the *Südhang* street and shortly thereafter left into *Hörnleweg*, which takes us out of the town. From here, we have a wonderful view of the mountain panorama with the Hörnle, and the Ammer Mountains in the background. We meet the main road, follow it for approx. 40 m to the left and then turn right at a small chapel into the meadow path. We follow the signs down a gentle decline in the direction of Bad Bayersoien.

We remain on this path and orient ourselves to the left in the direction of Lettigenbichl, shortly before the rise. We follow the signs for *Achrundweg*. We continue straight on at the fork into a mountain pine moor area typical for this landscape. Drainage ditches border our path on both sides.

We keep to the right at the next crossroads. We cross the stream accompanying us to the left at the next opportunity and hike uphill to the left. At the next crossroads, we keep to the left and soon thereafter we follow a footpath to the right, which brings us directly to the chapel hill (Kapellenberg) of Bad Bayersoien. From the memorial chapel (Gedächtniskapelle) we have a magnificent view of the entire town, the lake and the Ammergau Alps. We descend via steps once again, turn to the left and then again to the left into *Kirmesauer Straße*. A footpath to the right leads directly to the lake.

Lake Soier 3

On arrival, we follow the path around the lake. After almost circumnavigating the lake, we cross the inlet and proceed to the left along the stream back to the town road, which we follow to the right into the town centre.

St. Georg Parish Church

A church was mentioned for the first time in Bayersoien in 1315. We can however assume

that a church existed before this date. The exact construction date of the late Gothic hall church is unknown. The church was renewed and extended from 1717.

The Gothic chancel remained and the nave was built in the Baroque style. The stucco work was awarded to Joseph Schmuzer's workshop. The frescoes originate from Franz Seraph Zwinck from Oberammergau.

We leave Bad Bayersoien and take the *Dorfstraße* in a northerly direction until the intersection with *Ludwigstraße*. We follow this road to the left, cross over the B 23 and initially proceed in a curve to the right. Using the signpost, we orient ourselves to *Soyermühle*, which lies to the right. Where the residential road bends to the right, our path continues straight on, and we leave the town below the last houses.

After a short while our meadow path meets a tarred road, which we first follow for a few metres to the right. We then turn to the left soon afterwards. We follow a gentle decline to the left past the next clump of trees and then remain on this path until we reach the tree-covered banks of the Ammer. At the point where our path continues to the left, we take a narrow path to the right, which leads downwards in serpentines, mainly via steps.

Once we have reached the Ammer, we use the bridge to cross to the opposite side of the river. We then continue to the left at the Soyer mill. Our path now rises constantly until we reach a fork. The road to the right leads to an option for Hargenwies (this will be described below). We continue to the left through the spruce forest.

The path in front of us requires a great deal of attention. We follow the narrow path over small wooden bridges and a large number of tree roots. Our high position allows us to enjoy the wonderful views of the Ammer from time to time.

Our path winds along, sometimes with steps, down to the level of the river again. We continue along a gravel bank down the river. The climbing is gentle at first but becomes steeper until we reach a clearing. Our journey is then to the left through this clearing.

The effort was worth it, as from here we have a breath-taking view of the Ammer, bubbling far beneath us. We descend from here, once again relatively steeply via steps until we finally reach the river banks. We then continue in a straight line to the Schleierfälle waterfall – a natural landmark. We keep right however, and follow the signpost to *Hargenwies*. From here, we once again have a view down to the river, although we soon need to

overcome a steep climb. We finally come to an information board at the top, and meet a forestry road, where we turn left towards Kammerl.

Option via Hargenwies:
At the fork after the Soyer mill we follow the rise to the right through the wood and then continue to the left at the next crossroads shortly before a clearing along the fringes of the wood down to the hamlet of Kreut (865 m). We continue in a straight line to a crossroads, where we turn to the left and then need to walk approx. 1 km along the little-used Morgenbach – Hargenwies connecting road. In front of us is a beautiful view of the Hörnle peaks.

In Hargenwies we orient ourselves to the left at the sign towards the Schleierfälle and follow this approx. 500 m along a meadow path. At the beginning of the forest we pass a culvert. We then keep right and walk along a clearing to a crossroads with the Ammer gorge information board. From here we can descend to the Schleierfälle or continue walking along the forest road towards Kammerl.

We now remain on this path, which climbs gently through the wood until we reach a clearing. We then continue to the left along the edge of the wood, crossing over a wooden bridge and reach another clearing after passing through a section of the woods. We go along this clearing to the left and cross a bridge, before walking through part of a spruce wood. We then encounter a cross in the field at the next clearing. We need to take care when descending from here to the Ammer. The concrete stones and steps can be slippery. After crossing via an iron bridge, we arrive directly at the Kammerl power station.

Kammerl Power Station (Kraftwerk Kammerl)

The power station was constructed in 1896 by Kummer und Co. Dresden AG for supplying the rail link between Murnau and Oberammergau. In 1904 Siemens was awarded the contract to renew the generators, and in 1938 ownership of the power station passed to the German Imperial Railways (Deutsche Reichsbahn) and later the German Federal Railways (Deutsche Bundesbahn). The conversion to automatic operation was performed in October 1980. Since then the facility has been controlled remotely from Munich.

The Kammerl power station is the world's oldest railway power station still in operation for generating single-phase alternating current at a low frequency. Today it belongs to Deutsche Bahn AG.

We continue to the right past the railway power system that is over 100 years old, and proceed down to the Ammer bridge. This leads to the river bank on the opposite side.

Shortly after the next information board, a signboard invites us to follow a path to the left towards *Scheibum.*

Scheibum 4

We enter the forest, keeping left at the next fork and then take the narrow path to the right at the point where the road leads to the gravel bank of the Ammer. After a few steps, this path takes us to an observation platform. Let us take some time here to marvel at the unique natural Scheibum breach.

We now once again leave the Scheibum behind us and walk through the wood back to the Ammer bridge. We proceed to the left up along the tarred road and after a few minutes we reach the Acheleschwaig Inn with the old stabling facilities for the former state stud farm.

Acheleschwaig

The name of this village is derived from a combination of the words Ache, Lana and Schwaige, and means something like "Cattle yard on the slopes of the Ammer". The existence of the property was first confirmed in 1371, and it was owned for many centuries by the Ettal monks. Some years after the dissolution of the cloisters, a royal foaling yard was established here. This was owned by the Schwaiganger military stud farm. At the beginning of the 20th century, the Bavarian government took over the property and used it for breeding horses. A switch to breeding cattle was made in 1945, and from 1967 to 2006 the facility was used for research into breeding cattle.

Shortly after this estate, we turn left off the street onto an agricultural road. We immediately take then the road that leads to the left to Böhmerweiher. We climb gently over meadows, and then walk a short distance through a wood, and then right at a crossing. After 100 m the wood opens, and we find ourselves in the extremely idyllic Böhmerweiher. We continue our journey, arrive at a crossing at which we proceed to the right and enjoy a wonderful view over the Hörnle. This high route soon brings us to Saulgrub.

Fatima Chapel (Fatimakapelle) 5

Shortly before the village, and after a broad curve to the left, a meadow path leads to the left to the Fatima Chapel. We return to our trail path, turn to the left and then meet another crossroads. At this point the old Roman

View of the Ammer Mountains from Saulgrub

road in a sunken road leads us to the right, down to Saulgrub. At the *Dorfstraße* we turn left and arrive at the Church of St. Francis (Franziskuskirche).

Church of St. Francis (Franziskuskirche)

The village church was built by the inhabitants of Saulgrub in a single summer in 1859. The method of construction has similarities to the Gothic style. In August 1860 the church was consecrated to Saint Francis of Assisi.

We continue along the *Dorfstraße* and arrive at the traffic lights, intersecting with the heavily used main road. We first walk along the pavement for a short while and cross the street at the point where the path on the opposite side of the street leads us away from the street again through the Kirchfeld district. In the residential area, we turn into the third street that we meet on the right.

A gentle decline leads us to the Saulgrub mill, which we pass on the left hand side before reaching the other side of the stream via an iron bridge. At the next intersection, we turn to the left and then keep right at the next fork. After another 100 m we turn right again and find ourselves in the Bad Kohlgrub peat cut Rochusfeld after a few steps.

Rochusfeld 6

A bench reminds us of the authoress Adele Gerhard's favourite place – a place where she often spent time relaxing in Bad Kohlgrub. We continue straight ahead until we reach a peat hut on the left hand side. We return to *Adele-Gerhard-Weg*, proceed into the town and follow the railway line for a short while until we reach the St. Rochus chapel.

In the Ludwigs Gorge of Bad Kohlgrub

St. Rochus Chapel (Rochuskapelle)

In the wake of the Thirty Years' War, Bad Kohlgrub also did not remain unscathed by the plague in 1632 and 1633. In 1635 the remaining inhabitants built this votive chapel in thanks on the plague cemetery. The chapel was consecrated to Rochus, one of the saints who protected against the plague, and it was approximately the size of the current chancel.

The chapel soon became too small for the number of pilgrims. In 1733 it was extended by a new construction by the Wessobrunn artist Joseph Schmuzer. The interior of the light roofed hall is preserved in the finest Rococo stucco.

We proceed to the right past the cemetery down to the railway line, cross over, hike a short way to the right and then continue to follow *St.-Rochus-Straße* to the left. We remain on this street even after crossing the town thoroughfare, and come upon a street that takes us to the left to the parish church of Bad Kohlgrub.

St. Martin Parish Church (Pfarrkirche St. Martin)

A small Martin chapel has probably existed on this site since the early Middle Ages. The construction of the current church began around 1342 and was commissioned by the provost of Rottenbuch at that time. Numerous extensions took place in the years that followed.

The current configuration of the church originated from the years between 1722 and 1729. The late Middle Ages tower was raised between 1750 and 1755, and crowned with a Baroque steeple. The interior is designed in the early Rococo style, and is at least partially the work of the Rottenbuch cloister architect Joseph Schmuzer.

We continue on our journey and reach the *Hauptstraße* again. We orient ourselves to the right in the direction of village troug and walk past the town hall into the spa park of the peat spa resort. In the park we take the path that leads to the left past the music pavilion and makes a curve to the right behind the water-treading basin. We then cross a steel bridge and leave the spa park again to the left, following the gently rising *Mythenpfad* to the right. To the right in front of us, we discover a newly erected stone circle, and continue to climb alongside a stream. Wind chimes hang from a tree above our heads.

From the height that we have now attained, we can enjoy a beautiful view over the Murnau moor and the mountains behind it, all the way to the Benediktenwand.

We follow our path and gently descend into the Ludwig Gorge. We then climb over steps and bridges, past numerous waterfalls and leave the ravine once more via steps.

At the top, we continue to the right along the field path and at the second intersection we turn left up to the parking area for the Tannenbankerl lift. Behind a wooden hut, located to the right above us, we cross over the ski run and reach a footpath that takes us up to the Sonnen district.

We pass the fire-fighting water tanks and continue on the right until we reach a large crossing, where we continue to the left. Behind the parking area of a spa hotel, we follow the tarred road down to the right to the hamlet of Kraggenau. At the first farm the path turns to the left and then soon gently rises until we reach a hill with a wonderful view over the local Unterammergau mountains Pürschling and Teufelstättkopf that lie in front of us.

We then descend on a path through a small wooded area. We find a wider tarred road, where we continue to the left. We are once again on the *Alte Römerstraße* and follow it for a short time until we reach the next village Wurmansau.

Wurmansau Chapel (Kapelle Wurmansau)

The little church with its patron, Saint Joseph, was built in 1779. The ceiling artwork from the year 1780 depicts the marriage of Mary. Older still, from around 1700, is a work depicting Bishop Conrad. It reminds us of the hermit Conrad, who lived here in the 17th century, and who was reputedly killed by the plundering hordes.

We cross straight through the village, pass the Inn Ammertaler Hof and leave via *Wiesmahdweg*. The path now winds parallel to the main road in a southerly direction below the Hörnle, with a view over the Ammer Valley and the Ammergau Alps. At a crossing, a signpost points to the left, towards Hörnle cabin, but we continue straight on. After a curve to the right, we cross a wide wooden bridge and turn immediately to the left onto a path. A stream flows towards us on the left side. We come to a crossroads, orient ourselves at this point to the right and see the Kappel Church. On the tarred road that leads away from the church to the left, we come across a pond on the right hand side, and then reach the Lourdes Grotto via a footpath.

Lourdes Grotto (Lourdesgrotte)

On 28 July 1919 this grotto was inaugurated. It commemorates apparitions of the Virgin Mary experienced by Bernadette Soubirous in Lourdes. The town in the Pyrenees has since been the most popular and most visited destination for Marian pilgrimages in Europe.

After leaving the grotto we walk on a small path, leading up to the Kappel church as a way of the cross.

Kappel Church 7

It is estimated that the Kappel Church was founded in 1090. It is thus the mother church of the Ammer Valley. At an even earlier date, there is said to have been a hermitage of Eticho the Welf on this site. He died around 910. In the 15th century, a Gothic

On the Hoernle

chapel stood here. The tower stems from this period. Due to the increase in pilgrims, the church was enlarged in the 17th century and the inner hall was decorated with Rococo stucco ornaments by Franz Xaver Schmuzer the following century.

In order to keep the old tradition of the Pilgrimage of the Holy Blood alive, the Kappel Church has been the destination of the Unterammergau Leonhardi procession since 1963.

Coming from the portal we keep to the right and come back to our hiking trail through a large wooden gate. After the cattle pen we do not follow the sign pointing towards the Hörnle cabin, instead take the slightly climbing trail through the meadow straight ahead towards Hörnle.

Hörnle 8

At the next fork in the path, we take the right and pass a wooden gate. We now continue uphill and have many wonderful views down into the valley and the Pulvermoos nature reserve.

Following the climbing, we soon come to a wider path and to a fork at the end of a clearing. To the right a path leads to the *Hinteres Hörnle*, but we ascend straight ahead through the forest until we can see the summit cross of the *Mittleres Hörnle*. Arriving at the peak, we stop to enjoy the unique panorama surrounding us.

We head down in northwesterly direction and in the valley follow a trail that leads us below the *Vorderes Hörnle* to the Hörnle cabin.

From the cabin, we take the same path that we came on. We do not climb the *Mittleres Hörnle*, but stay on the path to the left of the peak. Then we descend slightly for a short way before climbing again towards the *Hinteres Hörnle*. At the next fork, we keep to the right and follow the relatively flat trail to the *Stierkopf*. Here again, we do not go over the peak, but stay on the trail to the right of it. We enjoy a beautiful view of Unterammergau.

After circling the *Stierkopf*, we again descend slightly over mountain pastures to the edge of a wood. A relatively steep path begins here that takes us down serpentine paths through the spruce forest. At the end of this descent, we reach the Drei Marken crossroads. We are 1263 metres above sea level and follow the signs to Oberammergau via Romanshöhe.

The wide forestry road now goes mostly downhill. At the next fork, we keep to the right and pass a log cabin to the left of the path. Soon thereafter, we go straight ahead just before a gate and stay on this path until the next fork, where we take the right and continue down.

We now come to a clearing at the right of the path and immediately after that, we have to walk down through a very steep ravine. At the bottom, we reach *Altherrenweg*, where we turn left and soon arrive at the Romanshöhe Inn.

To our right are fabulous views of the Ammer Valley and the mountains of Oberammergau lying opposite us: Kolben and Kofel. We now continue downhill on an asphalt road. Before a bridge, we leave this road and take a path that leads alongside a brook.

When we arrive at the next tarred road, we turn left, cross the bridge, and continue to Oberammergau. From *Warbergstraße* we take the second right at *In die Furch* and then come to *Theaterstraße*. If we follow this street to the right again, we soon stand in front of the large building housing the Oberammergau Passion Play Theatre.

Passion Play Theatre (Passionstheater) 9

The first time the Passion Play was staged here on the *Passionswiese* was 1830. Before that, the cemetery next to the village church was used. The simple wooden stage was equipped with backdrops and stage equipment. In 1890, a new half-timbered style stage was built on steel arch girders. Not until 1930 was the wood construction replaced by stone. At the same time, theatre seats were put in the auditorium to replace the simple wooden benches. In May 2008, a mobile roof of steel and synthetics over the stage was installed.

We continue on our way heading south, cross the *Dorfstraße* and walk a few steps straight ahead to House of Pontius Pilate.

The open air stage in the Passion Play Theatre Oberammergau

House of Pontius Pilate (Pilatushaus) and Lüftlmalerei

The House of Pontius Pilate was built in 1784 and is considered the most beautiful of all of the fresco-painted houses in Oberammergau. It represents the climax of Baroque house painting in the town and was done by Franz Seraph Zwinck. The fresco depicts Jesus Christ in front of Pontius Pilate and the high priests, the resurrection of Christ, and architectural murals.

Lüftlmalerei is a special form of façade painting popular in the 18th century. The most famous painter was the Oberammergau church

The House of Pontius Pilate

painter Franz Seraph Zwinck (1748 – 1792). To make the paintings more durable, he used the already known fresco technique, i.e. painting using fresh plaster.

He called himself a *"Lüftlmaler"* (air painter) as a description of his rapid technique. The fresh mountain air dried out the plaster quickly, making it necessary to work fast.

We take *Verlegergasse* past House of Pontius Pilate in southwesterly direction, cross *Eugen-Papst-Straße* and reach the bank of the river Ammer on *Pürschlingweg*. The bridge takes us to the other side, where we turn to the right and almost immediately then left again on a path. After curving around to the left, the path begins to ascend slowly.

We come to a street and follow this to the right to Osterbichl. We gradually leave the last few houses behind and in a few minutes reach the monumental crucifixion scene.

Monument of Crucifixion (Kreuzigungsgruppe) 10

From this height, we enjoy again a lovely view of the Passion Play village. The path now takes us over the Kolben ski slope to *Grottenweg*. We hike along this trail along the rock walls of *Kofel* Mountain. After a few minutes, we discover numerous petroglyphs in the rock named *Mahlenstein* that possibly stem from Roman times. A bit further on, on the wall of *Langer Kofel*, we see more petroglyphs that presumably stem from the 18th and 19th centuries. We remain on this trail and discover a shrine to St. Mary near the cemetery at the foot of the steep face. Going further down this trail, we now reach a higher plateau, the *Kälberplatte*. Across from us, a wooden sign points the way to *Döttenbichl*.

We follow the climbing to the left into the woods up to a rise. A short way after that we head downhill again, the trail is partially marked by a yellow dagger, until we reach the excavation site with information signs.

Döttenbichl 11

Excavations from the years 1992 to 1997 allow the assumption that a Celtic fire sacrifice site was located on this wooded hill. The numerous finds included Celtic fibulae, iron bowls and numerous, mostly agricultural, tools. In addition, coins, three daggers, over 300 arrowheads, and shoe tacks from Roman soldiers were found.

Three catapult arrowheads can be allocated to the 19th Roman legion, which was defeated totally in *Teutoburg Forest* in the

year 9 AD. We assume that they crossed the Alps twenty-four years earlier, in 15 BC, and fought the Celtic people who were living here.

We return to *Kälberplatte* on the same trail. Turning right downhill, we follow the ravine and keep to the left. At the northern part of the large bridge a footpath leads us up to the highway and across the bridge heading south. At the end of this highway, we leave it and pass under the bridge. We keep to the left and continue our way following the Ammer upriver.

At the next crossroads, we turn left and pass through an underpass to arrive at the edge of Oberammergau. Here we follow the signs to *Vogelherdweg*, cross the access road and approach the rock wall below the Laber. Now we have to turn left along the highway for a few minutes.

We see the so-called Bear Cave with a statue of St. Mary up towards the left in the rock wall and shortly thereafter take the uphill path to the left between the trees.

picture on the left: View from the Weidmoos towards Laber

We continue uphill on a forest path until we reach a fork, where we keep to the left, and after a few paces, see our first view of Ettal. At halfway, the *Vogelherdweg* takes us above the town and the abbey. Through the trees, we catch more views of part of the large Benedictine Abbey of Ettal.

Abbey of Ettal (Kloster Ettal) 12

Founded in 1330 by Emperor Ludwig the Bavarian, the cloister and the knight's academy were opened in 1332. The emperor was apparently inspired to establish this unusual monastery by the epic "Parzival" by Wolfram von Eschenbach.

The centre of the monastery was a statue of St. Mary made of white marble that the emperor had brought from Italy. After the 15th century, but especially in the 17th century, Ettal was the site of great pilgrimages. In the large fire in 1744, the Gothic church, the knight academy and part of the monastery were destroyed. Reconstruction was done in Rococo style by the master builder and stuccoer Joseph Schmuzer from Wessobrunn.

After secularization in 1803, it was almost one hundred years before the abbey was returned to its original purpose on August 6, 1900.

A good way behind the utility buildings of the abbey, we turn right at *Ettaler Manndl Weg*, pass the town's water reservoir, and take the next right.

Going straight ahead, we come to the abbey building and enter the courtyard through the second arch on the left. To our left, we see the mighty Baroque portal of the church.

We leave the courtyard through the southern arch. Opposite us on the other side of the street, a path leads out of the town. We walk across a flat meadow to the edge of a wood. Here we keep to the right and follow the signs to the Ettal mill. Before reaching it, we pass the village's water treatment plant and cross a street.

Ettal Mill (Ettaler Mühle)

In 1701, the mill was built as a sawmill by the monastery. After secularization there were many new owners. Today it is the monastery's property again.

Behind the inn, we continue left into the Weidmoos nature preserve. Our path leads us along the river Ammer straight ahead to an asphalt road. We turn left and walk down this road a bit, cross the street and take the hiking trail opposite us that takes us near the little Ammer springs.

Ammer springs (Ammerquellen)

Walking on *Sonnenweg* along Dickenwald, we reach the farms of the hamlet of Rahm. We stay on this path until we reach Graswang.

Graswang

The word "wang" indicates that the name stems from Germanic times. "Wang" meant a green area, an ideal pasture. The village was probably inhabited before Ettal. The first records of the community mention five cattle farms in 1280.

To get to the village, we turn left and come to the Maria Schutz Church where we rest a while.

Maria Schutz Church (Kirche Maria Schutz)

It was built in 1954 and has a 30 m high steeple. The statues are by Ludwig Huber, Oberammergau sculptor and former director of the wood carving school. The altar features a statue of the Virgin Mary, to her right and left are villagers: farmer, woodcutter, hunter, priest, mothers, and children.

On the dais are images of the 14 Stations of the Cross and the 14 Holy Helpers. In the middle is a depiction of the Madonna of Ettal.

The hamlet Graswang with the Church Maria Schutz

On the other side of the street, the trail leads to the forester's lodge in Dickelschwaig. From afar we can already see the Chapel of Holy Gertrudis next to the forester's lodge.

Dickelschwaig 14

The Schwaige (a kind of farm) was almost always a monastery institution and was managed by an administrator. In 1812 it became the property of the king and was made a branch of the royal Schwaiganger horse-breeding farm. In summer, 50 to 80 young horses from the military stud farm were pastured here. It later changed hands frequently. In 1929, the Oberammergau Forestry Service acquired the estate. Today, it houses a branch of that office.

We are now at an altitude of about 1000 m and to the left of the trail, we reach the entry gate to the Linderhof Palace Garden. We now walk down royal pathways for a while, keeping to the left at the first fork and left again at the one after that. We follow the sign to *"Hundinghütte"* which we then see next to a pond before us after a right curve. Just a few steps further to the left of the trail is Ludwig II's next retreat, the *"Gurnemanz-Klause"*.

A path now leads to the right up the slope through the woods. The trail continues to climb until we reach our destination at the highest point of the ridge. Across from us is the Venus Temple at the highest point of the terraces that lead straight down to the royal villa.

Linderhof Palace 15

In order to enlarge the forestry lodge of his father, Maximilian II., in 1869 King Ludwig II. purchased the area around the farmhouse of what was then the Linderhof farm. Initially he had his hunting lodge rebuilt to a "king's cabin". But in 1870, a larger addition was built and then several more phases of construction in the following years. In 1878, the royal villa was completed. In the last phase in 1885, the bedroom was enlarged.

Carl Joseph von Effner, the Munich court garden director, designed the large palace park. The grounds were landscaped with terraced gardens with a Venus Temple, several bridges and waterfalls and various buildings. Among them are the Moorish Kiosk, the Moroccan House and the Venus Grotto. This artificial grotto with illuminated lake and waterfall is said to have reminded the king of the Wagnerian opera "Tannhäuser".

His love of Richard Wagner's operas can also be seen in the building of the Hundinghütte modeled after the opera "Valkyrie" and the Gurnemanz retreat from the third act of "Parsifal".

Linderhof was the only palace planned by King Ludwig II. that he lived to see completed.

Linderhof Palace

Sponsors of the Meditation Trail

Gemeinde Steingaden

passionsspiele 2010
oberammergau

Gemeinde Rottenbuch

MoorSymphonie
Wellness- und Gesundheitsurlaub in Bayern

DAS POSCH HOTEL

www.poschhotel.de
Telefon: +49(0) 8822.922 100

Natur
GASTGEBER
AMMERGAUER ALPEN

Ammergauer Alpen
Die Schaukäserei

Fux

*Ferienhaus Fux - Hotel Garni****
Mannagasse 2a - 82487 Oberammergau
www.firmafux.de

KRÄUTER PÄDAGOGE™

Annemarie Gerold und Martin Unruh

Integrative Körperarbeit
Norbert Parucha

Kreissparkasse
Garmisch-Partenkirchen
Fair. Menschlich. Nah.

ammerquellen.de

Kur- und Verkehrsverein
Bad Kohlgrub

VERKEHRSVEREIN BAD BAYERSOIEN

FRAUENLISTE
OBERAMMERGAU E.V.

Verkehrsverein Saulgrub

Genoveva Fischer

OBERAMMERGAU MUSEUM

Frau von Mücke

ROTARY INTERNATIONAL
Rotary Club
Murnau-Oberammergau

Die Stöcke mit dem ganz persönlichen Design
brückl
HEILAND

Ettaler
Kloster-Liqueure

Symbolism of the 15 stations

The number 14 is a significant numeral in the Christian tradition. We know of 14 holy helpers, 14 patron saints and 14 stations of Jesus' cross.

We would like to take this a step further with the 15 stations of the Ammergau Alps Meditation Trail. The French town of Lourdes, the centre of Marian pilgrimage was also provided an additional station to the traditional 14 stations of the cross many years ago.

Jesus' life of suffering certainly also ends there with the entombment, but he receives redemption at the additional station. The 15th station, the empty grave, symbolises his resurrection; the rolling away of the tombstone signifies the rising sun, the light for the world.

Our stations are based on the Latin word "statio". The Catholic church sees this to mean a place in which people meet for a pilgrimage or a procession. The "statio" is a place for reflection and silent prayer.

Monument of Crucifixion

Information centres

www.brennendes-herz.com

Ammergau Alps

Tourist Information Oberammergau
Eugen-Papst-Straße 9a
82487 Oberammergau
Tel. +49 (0)88 22/92 27 40
www.oberammergau.de

Kur- und Tourist Information Bad Bayersoien
Dorfstraße 45
82435 Bad Bayersoien
Tel. +49 (0)88 45/70 30 62-0
www.bad-bayersoien.de

Kur- und Tourist Information Bad Kohlgrub
Im Haus der Kurgäste
82433 Bad Kohlgrub
Tel. +49 (0)88 45/74 22-0
www.bad-kohlgrub.de

Tourist Information Ettal
Ammergauer Straße 8
82488 Ettal
Tel. +49 (0)88 22/35 34
www.ettal.de

Tourist Information Saulgrub
Kohlgruber Straße 2
82442 Saulgrub
Tel. +49 (0)88 45/10 66
www.saulgrub.de

Tourist Information Altenau
Obere Dorfstraße 25
82442 Altenau
Tel. +49 (0)88 45/18 81
www.altenau-bayern.de

Tourist Information Unterammergau
Dorfstraße 23
82497 Unterammergau
Tel. +49 (0)88 22/64 00
www.unterammergau.de

!

Emergency numbers: from landline 19222, from mobile phones 112

Alpine weather conditions hotline: +49 (0)89/29 50 70

For information on **accommodation, public parking areas or public transport** (bus and train) please contact the local tourist information (p. 83)

Image credits

Ammergauer Alpen GmbH p. 43, 69; Ammergauer Alpen GmbH, Siegfried Karpf p. 39, 41, 47, 57, 82; Ammergauer Alpen GmbH, Daniela Blöchinger p. 27, 58; Ammergauer Alpen GmbH, Matthias Neubauer, p. 18, 50, 54, 60; Ammergauer Alpen GmbH, Eberhard Starosczik, p. 6, 8, 10, 12-13, 17, 25, 29, 33, 35, 43, 45, 62; Ammergauer Alpen GmbH, Hans-Peter Schöne p. 77; Ammergauer Alpen GmbH, Alois Schindler p. 65; Ammergauer Alpen GmbH, Bad Kohlgrub p. 31; Ammergauer Alpen GmbH, Oberammergau Tourismus p. 14, 37, 72, 74; Bayerische Schlösserverwaltung, www.schloesser.bayern.de, www.linderhof.de, p. 49, 79; Pfarramt Wieskirche, Christoph Schneider p. 21, 53; Pfarrei Rottenbuch, Erwin Reiter, p. 23; Timberland-Trail p. 66; Passionsspiele Oberammergau 2000 p. 71

Disclaimer

The information provided in this brochure has been researched with utmost care. Notwithstanding, errors cannot be completely ruled out, as we have to point out in the context of product liability regulations. Therefore all information is provided without obligations or guarantees on behalf of the Ammergauer Alpen GmbH or the authors. Both do not assume responsibility or liability for any discrepancies in the content. Utilization of the information occurs at the user's own risk. There is no liability for accidents happening due to the route descriptions or the conditions of the routes. We ask for your understanding for this disclaimer and are always open for advice on useful amendments.

Unfortunately we could not identify the entitled persons for all quotations used in this publication. We ask holders of rights to contact the Ammergauer Alpen GmbH, providing proof of ownership.